First the Egg

Laura Vaccaro Seeger

A Neal Porter Book

ROARING BROOK PRESS

New Milford, Connecticut

First

the EGG

then

the CHICKEN

First

the TADPOLE

then

the FROG

First

the SEED

then

the FLOWER

First

the CATERPILLAR

then

the BUTTERFLY

with,not?vKnoqeanow

qNthenvg;yesDpanlk

wow!ifjorkbigzeh,bay

girl;axhowgdownEjrfr

;whoJpa**First**na,thatn

Can;butAethej!whatfkj

nhere?goodjn!fbwhenj

lswinogb,qare;wherea

from,oh!ptwhyV;badS

mz,jhsWthereohim?rh

the W▮▮D

the STORY

Once upon a time
there was an egg
and a chicken and a
tadpole and a frog
and a seed and a
flower and a
caterpillar and a
butterfly and...

First

the PAINT

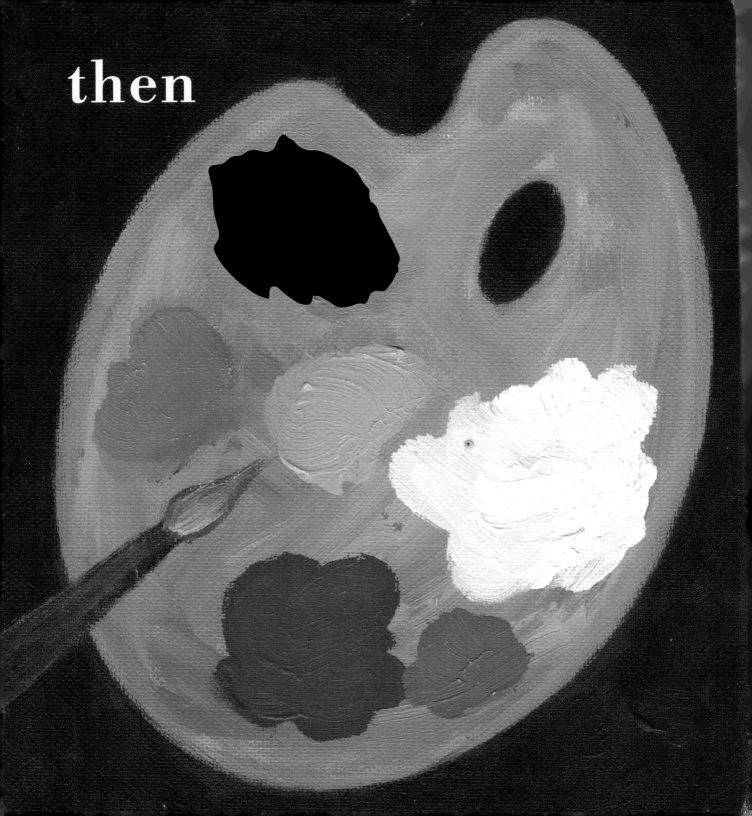

then

the PICTURE . . .

First
the CHICKEN

then

the EGG!

for Chris